Bruno Pisano LaV1, Inc.

(888) 95 BRUNO * (888) 952-7866

info@lav1.com

Contents

Praise for Bruno Pisano..1

Preface 4

Introduction 6

How do you know if you need local SEO?....................................7

Local SEO Checklist...8

Keyword Selection..8

On-Site SEO 11

Off-Site SEO 13

Local Directory Listings..13

Citations 14

Delete Duplicate Listings & Citations.......................................16

Content Marketing...17

Encourage Customer Reviews 18

Social Media...19

Be Mobile Ready 20

Online Videos 21

Regularly Monitor, Tweak and Improve....................................22

SEO Factors: The Top 33 Signal Boosts....................................25

1. Place keywords at the beginning of your title.......................26

2. Make sure your URLs are Human and SEO Friendly...........27

3. Take your content beyond text..29

4. Don't post links, curate..30

5. Get to the topic in the first 100 words 31

6. Speed up your website. 32

7. Cultivate page authority and PageRank.................................33

8. Use the headline tag...34

9. Google's Domain Authority metric is important.....................35

10. Post long-form content. 36

11. Use strategic placement of keywords and related topics. 37

12. Use modifiers that people use in searches................................38

13. Make social media sharing easy...39

14. Design your site for mobile access..40

15. Kill your bounce rate. 41

16. Keep users around. 42

17. Mention related keywords and subtopics. 43

18. Weed out weak and duplicate content.....................................44

19. Content matters. 45

20. Link to your own website. 46

21. Use headings and subheadings..47

22. Optimize images...48

23. Ensure your inbound links are relevant...................................49

24. Schema.org microformats provide extra information to search engines. 50

25. Use the tools that Google and Bing give you! 51

26. Use an XML sitemap..52

27. Use YouTube videos. 53

28. Don't forget the terms of use statement and privacy policy......55

29. Build secure sites whenever possible. 56

30. Leave breadcrumbs for your visitors.......................................57

31. Reviews and reputation influencers impact your SERPs. 58

32. Be user friendly and break up content. 59

33. Set canonical links. 60

Conclusion 61

Praise for Bruno Pisano

"Bruno is a driven artist who has brought his graphic skills into the modern age for Web design work. His smiling, able attitude make for great hits, both for our Web Design as well as in online ads for his outreach efforts in local and international organizations. Bruno is a true winner, and his dedication and devotion to an honest and art worthy life make him a valuable asset to my team."

Zack Smith, A&M Corporation

"Bruno brought us on par with our competitors in only a matter of months. We saw an increase in our traffic and thus started fulfilling orders like crazy. I can't thank him enough for our new found success. He comes highly recommended anytime someone asks me about my SEO initiatives."

Ciaran Redmond, American Sentinel University

"Bruno is a true professional. He knows SEO and digital marketing. I highly recommend him. He has a professional attitude and a get it done mentality. It you have an SEO project and you want it done correctly, on time, and on budget than you need to work with Bruno and his team!"

Gregg Towsley, Marketing Consultant and Rainmaker

"Bruno is one of the industry's premier search engine optimization (SEO) experts! He's extremely knowledgeable with the leading marketing tactics that really work (not simply employing old, tired strategies like the other guys) to get you the visitors you need for your site(s). Not only is Bruno one of the friendliest and most personable guys you'll ever meet, he's also trustworthy and totally motivated to your success. I highly recommend Bruno for any web/social media marketing and SEO projects!"

Sean Hudson, Technician

 "SEO is more than just words on a page. You need video too to get the ranks. Bruno understands how important a good, short and punchy video is. He set everything up for me, directed, edited and provided the script. Thanks to Bruno, my business is growing. Having an Internet page is important for business today. Being able to get on Page 1 of Google's search results is just as important. Bruno can put you on the front page, but only if you call him!"

Sean Christopher Rush, Aerial Rush Photography and Survey

 "Bruno has been an absolute blessing to deal with. Not only did he help our firm enhance our website but he also increased our presence on the internet by getting us on the first page of Google/Bing. His ability to break concepts down and help us see the end goal was invaluable. Thanks to him we've added new customers and increased sales. He definitely knows SEO and is more than capable of helping any business. Thanks again!"

John Knowles, CMS Customer Solutions

Preface

I studied Computer Programming and graduated from UCLA in 1995. Spent a year and a half learning, C, C++, COBOL, DOS, and so many other languages that I actually… never, EVER used!

Was it a waste of time?

Not a bit! While there, one of my classmates, an Indian fellow whose initials were B.S. (and he was an honest to God guy!), alerted me that "there's this thing called "The Internet", and the future of business will change forever". He urged me to get on the bandwagon, and I saw the opportunity.

I studied HTML and started creating webpages for friends that owned local stores, for very cheap, until they started making a lot of money online selling their goods from my work… soon I realized I can make a career from helping businesses achieve online success. I wanted to learn as much as it was possible to be the leader in the industry.

Fast forward to now, August 2015, and in this, my first book on sharing what REALLY works when it comes to Internet Marketing, and being in the first page of the searches, I want to uncover all the things that you need to DO, in order to beat your competition online.

Back to 1995, with the still hopes to play professional soccer in the newly formed MLS, I quickly found out that the elements that an athlete takes to succeed on the pitch, are the same that someone in business must use: planning, persistence, teamwork, positivism, attitude, etc.

I'm very proud of my achievements, and I'm happy that you're reading this copy.

If you ever need any kind of help from me, feel free to contact me at your convenience.

Enjoy your reading!

Bruno Pisano

Director, LaV1, Inc.

Introduction

If your company has a website, chances are you know a little something about Search Engine Optimization (SEO.) Since the early days of the internet, web designers and business owners have done whatever they can to guarantee their website is at (or near) the top of search results for chosen keywords.

As Google's search algorithms get more sophisticated, though, they began to custom-tailor results to suit the preferences of the user – and that includes geographical location. That's where local SEO comes in. It's the process of optimizing your website to get a higher "local" search ranking.

Oftentimes, Google users enter geo-targeted keywords to find local businesses - such as "best chiropractor in Los Angeles." If you are a chiropractor in Los Angeles, you want your clinic to show up high on that results list, and that's why local SEO is important.

It differs from regular SEO in a few key ways:

- Regular SEO is about building authority for a website (which may or may not include geographical information); local SEO is about establishing reliability for a business that exists in a particular physical location.

- Regular SEO relies heavily on backlinks to build credibility for a site in the eyes of the search engines; local SEO relies on citations that verify the business is real, as well as solidify their location.

- The goal of regular SEO is to rank organically high for chosen keywords; the goal of local SEO is to also break into the list of local search results.

How do you know if you need local SEO?

The answer to that question is very simple. If you own a brick and mortar store that relies on local customers to stay afloat, you need local SEO.

Most consumers today go online search engines to find local products, services, and businesses. In other words, many of your potential customers are looking for a place to buy via web search and your company isn't ranking well, you're missing out.

- Before we get into the Ultimate Blueprint, let's identify some of the key benefits of being in the first page:

- It helps generate traffic for both your website and your physical location

- It increase name recognition

- It helps build authority and credibility for your business

- It is easier to move up in a local search (if you do it right) than in organic search

- It can increase your return on investment (ROI) because you are spending marketing dollars where they will do the most good

- It increases conversions – companies that rank high for local search get more conversions because the people who see them on Google are a targeted audience

Now that you have a basic idea of what local SEO is and why you need it, let's get into the following Local SEO Checklist.

Local SEO Checklist

What do you need to do in order to successfully optimize your website for local search? Local SEO has many things in common with traditional SEO, so let's run them down.

Keyword Selection

The first step in any SEO strategy is to identify the best keywords for your business to target. A keyword is a search term or phrase entered by internet users to find information about a certain topic, product, service, or business.

Once they do, the search engine goes to work to find the best web pages to match the keyword; they also prioritize the list of results based on the best match for the keyword.

The good news is… coming up with a list of good keyword terms for local business is much easier than general SEO. It all boils down to location relevance and industry topic relevance.

For instance, let's say you're a divorce attorney in the Phoenix, AZ area. Obviously, you want people to find your business when they go online to search for "Phoenix divorce lawyers."

So by optimizing your site – and other online properties - for this keyword term, you have a better chance of showing up higher in the results. Although you can target multiple keywords throughout your website, it's best to start with only a few. If you focus on too many different keyword phrases in the beginning, you will wear yourself thin and it will be harder to get results.

To develop a list of keywords, first come up with a list of terms and phrases you think your target audience would use to find your type of business. Based on this list, you can do further research to choose the best keyword terms.

What geographical areas does your business serve?

How would people describe what your business provides?

What different products or services do you offer that could be used as search terms by consumers?

What type of problems does your business solve for consumers? What keywords are your competitors using in their SEO?

TIP: Don't be too general or broad with your keyword selections. It's important to use the right combinations of keyword variations in order to reach the right target audience. User intent has become a major search ranking factor. So when selecting your keywords, think about what a user is REALLY looking for when typing in that phrase.

For instance, a plumber may choose "leaking faucet" as a keyword. However, this may not be a good term to target because someone could simply be looking for information about fixing a leaking faucet themselves and not necessarily looking to hire a plumber.

However, if someone puts a city and/or state after a keyword term, they're likely looking to do business.

Keep in mind that searchers are becoming more and more specific with location-based searches. So be sure to localize your keyword phrases as much as possible to target specific areas. For instance, if your business is located in a suburban area of a major city, use keywords for that suburban town instead of trying to target the major city. Also feel free to hyper-target specific neighborhoods too if it works for your business.

You can also use the free Google AdWords Planner tool, as well as other keyword tools out there (some paid, some free) to check the number of searches and competition levels for each term. Due to the fact that this tool provides data based on whether there are advertisers for the selected keywords, it does not give you exact figures and should not be your only determining factor for keyword selection.

Another good resource for choosing your keywords is Google's suggested search terms; these are additional phrases that Google suggests in the search box as a user types in a particular keyword. They also give additional suggested terms at the bottom of the search results pages.

If you have Google Analytics on your website, this is another great resource to check to see which keyword terms are bringing in traffic currently.

On-Site SEO

Once you have identified keywords, the next step is to jump into on-site optimization – the things you can do on your website to help you rank for local searches:

- Include keywords (including geographical information) in key spots on your page: title tag, meta tags, alt image tags and even in the URL if you can.

- Create fresh and relevant content that includes your local keywords. Don't spam keywords – include them as an organic part of your content.

- Make sure your name, address and telephone number is embedded in the HTML code of every page.

- Include localization in blog posts and other content.

- Create a geo sitemap and KML file (keyhole markup language) that will allow your site to show up on Google Earth and Google Maps.

- Optimize logos and images with localized file names and alt tags.

- Blog about locally relevant topics.

Embed social media sharing buttons on your website.

Include information about your company's history and local roots on your "About Us" page.

Participate in (and blog about) local events.

Off-Site SEO

SEO also includes factors that aren't on your website:

- High quality backlinks from authoritative sites

- Content on video-sharing sites such as YouTube

- Content on social media

In order for these items to help you with local SEO, they have to include information like your location, as well as some of your important keyword terms.

Off-site optimization also includes several other key areas, which we will discuss in the following sections.

Local Directory Listings

Another important component of local SEO is getting your company listed in local directories.

- Sign up for Google My Business – this replaced Google Local

- Fill out your profile completely. Make sure to include:

  o Company name

  o Full address & phone number

- o Proper product & service categories

- o Photographs

- o Videos

- o Optimized description

- o Encourage customer reviews

- Sign up (or claim your business) on other directories, including Yahoo Local, Bing Local, Yelp and Angie's List

- Maintain a presence on location-specific social media, such as FourSquare, Citysearch and Mojopages

- Seek out industry-specific directories as well

Citations

Consistency does matter with local SEO, and nowhere is it more important than with listings of company name, address and phone number – also known as NAP citations. A NAP citation is not a link - it is merely a listing of your primary business information. Having a large number of accurate NAP citations is a huge part of getting your business to rank in local search results. Here are some things to keep in mind when collecting and monitoring citations:

- Get as many citations for your business as you can. A citation may include listings in directories like the ones mentioned above. However, other sources include:

o   Better Business Bureau

o   Local chambers of commerce

o   Yellow Pages

o   Local business directories

o   Horizontal directories like Yelp

o   Region-specific sites (www.Boston.com/places)

o   Industry-specific directories

o   Non-structured listings, such as those in local magazines or newspapers

- Be consistent when submitting your information. Even minor difference ("Street" instead of "St." or listings with and without a suite number) can impact your search ranking.

- Weed out duplicate listings

- Track down and correct inaccuracies

The goal is to have all of your NAP listings look exactly the same, because Google's algorithms will not be able to aggregate them.

Remember, the goal of local SEO is to give the location of your business credibility and authenticity. You can't do that if there are 10 different versions of your address out there. As you work your way through existing citations, keep a list of every place you are listed. That way in the future, if you change locations, you will be able to easily change your address when you need to.

Delete Duplicate Listings & Citations

As mentioned earlier, consistency is extremely important with local SEO. Google your business name or phone number and:

- Update addresses if you have moved

- Request that duplicates be removed

- Keep an eye out for fraudulent entries

If keeping track of online listing and citations has not been a priority, you may find that you are listed on cites where you need to log in. If that is the case and you do not remember your password, you may have to do a little extra work to get the listing corrected. Take the time to do it, because inaccuracies will be reflected in your local search ranking.

Content Marketing

Online content has become one of the most important factors for increasing brand visibility and influence online. Since 97% of consumers search for local businesses online, creating content tailored towards your specific target audience can be powerful for helping you get more traffic.

Content marketing is the practice of publishing interesting, useful, relevant content related to your industry online. The key here is to leave "selling" out of it and let your content do the selling for you in an indirect way. Instead, the focus should be on building relationships with your audience and establishing expert status in your industry. The overall goal is to engage your readers, which will help you convert those leads into customers.

- Define your target audience

- Choose your keywords

- Research topics for your content

  o Twitter Local Trends

  o Local News

  o Local Forums & Blogs

- Local Events

- Create a blog and post often

- Share content on social media

- Repurpose content into visual and rich media, such as videos, presentations, podcasts, images etc.

- Rinse and repeat for the long-term

Encourage Customer Reviews

Encourage your customers to review your business on Google+, Yelp or other review sites. The number of reviews you have has a direct impact on your Google placement. Here are a few things to keep in mind:

- Make sure to claim your business on all review sites and fill out a complete profile.

- Encourage reviews by putting logos for review sites on your page, or on your receipts.

- Make a point of responding to both positive and negative reviews.

- Suggest customers write reviews on a regular basis. It is better to have a steady stream of reviews than a huge flood of them.

Social Media

No local business can afford to overlook the importance of social media. That is as true of local SEO as it is of SEO in general. Here are a few things to keep in mind:

- Maintain an active presence on important social media sites, including Facebook, Google+, Twitter, LinkedIn, Pinterest, Instagram and YouTube. Note: Google+ is owned by Google. It is not as popular as Facebook, but having a presence there for your business is a must. Information and reviews on Google+ have a direct impact on your search rank.

- Fill out your profile and bio completely, and make sure to link back to your website.

- Have an editorial schedule that you stick to – having a Facebook page won't matter if you never update it. You need to keep your followers engaged.

- Use geo-specific keywords in your social media content. This will help you to optimize your social media content – and that will play a role in improving your rank in local search.

- Interact with other local business on social media.

- Follow relevant local organizations and events, such as your Chamber of Commerce, local farmers' markets, trade associations and fairs. Share their content when appropriate – and try to get them to share yours.

- Embed social sharing icons on your website.

Be Mobile Ready

More and more customers are accessing information about local businesses on their mobile devices. If your site is not already mobile- friendly, it should be. Here are some things to remember:

- On April 21, 2015 Google released a new algorithm to ascertain how mobile-friendly websites are. It was expected to have a significant impact on local mobile rankings.

- You can test your website by plugging the URL into Google's Mobile Friendly Test Tool

- Make sure the mobile version of your site is optimized for geo-specific keywords, just as your regular site is.

- Put an emphasis on getting the mobile version of your site to load quickly. Sites that load slowly (anything over 3 seconds is considered slow) have a high bounce rate – and your bounce rate can have an impact on your local search placement

- Think about including rich snippets – these are pieces of additional information such as your business hours, prices and products that can be coded to show up on under your page name in a list of search results.

- Design your mobile site for fat fingers. You want quality content, but it also needs to be easy to navigate on a small screen. Mobile users will get frustrated if things are too close together or difficult to read.

Online Videos

Videos are arguably the most popular kind of online content. A huge percentage of people watch videos online, and they are some of the most frequently-shared content. Creating and posting videos is a great way to boost your local SEO. Here are some tips:

- Post videos on your website, as well as on video sharing sites such as Youtube and Vimeo

- Geotag videos with your location information. YouTube makes this easy – all you need to do is go to Advanced Settings and search your location

- Include a link to your website in the description of the video

- Include your name, address and phone number in the frames at the end of the video – Google's algorithms will be able read the data, even when it is in video form

- Also include your NAP in the audio – Google produces a transcript of the video, so then your NAP will be included in the transcript

- Make full use of the opportunity to describe your video. In addition to a link to your website, include your NAP and a small bio or description of your business

- Associate the video with the Google+ page for your business

- Associate the video with your Google My Business page

- Embed the video on your website or blog

- Share the video on your social media pages and encourage others to share it as well

Regularly Monitor, Tweak and Improve

Once you have completed the local optimization of your site, it is important to be vigilant. Just as you would with regular SEO, you need to make a point of monitoring:

- Your citations and directory listings

- Your backlinks

- Your online reviews

- Your social media pages

If you standing in local search is not where you want it to be, you will need to continue tweaking your page and your off-site links and social media to improve your standing. Some things that may help you to improve include:

- Doing a user experience audit of your website – both the web and mobile versions

- Get your page to load more quickly

- Conduct ongoing keyword research

- Review traffic and tweak keywords as needed

- Do split testing of various components of your site

- Read Google's guidelines and best practices

Keeping your site optimized for local SEO is not a one-time thing. It requires an ongoing effort on your part. You can take steps now to get things started, but then it makes sense to have a regular schedule for monitoring your online presence.

The Ultimate Checklist

SEO Factors: The Top 33 Signal Boosts

It can be a frustrating task trying to find a single collection of SEO advice. Many search engine optimization articles focus on a small handful of factors. Noticing it made me set out to write all of short tips and hints that I wish I knew when first starting out. Because it could be an endlessly sprawling list, I decided to focus on the top 33 SEO factors that provide a signal boost in the SERPs (search engine results placement).

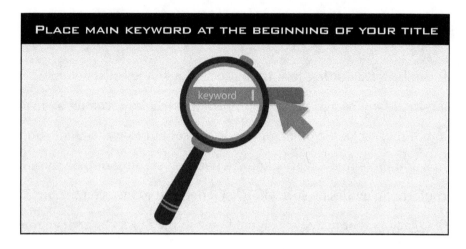

1. Place keywords at the beginning of your title.

Make sure your page title and title tag are placed at the beginning. Titles that start with relevant keywords, or mention them within a few words, perform best in search engine results. Both MO and Google data and reports detail this performance difference. Titles with relevant keywords near the beginning also have higher click through rates. Getting to the point about the topic tells potential visitors whether you have the content they are seeking.

2. Make sure your URLs are Human and SEO Friendly.

Pretty permalinks, or SEO-friendly URLs, are a standard tool used to make page addresses more attractive to both users and search engines. The flip side is ugly URLs, which are poor for SEO and social media sharing purposes. A pretty URL is simple and easily recognized, such as: randomexample.com/on-page-seo. A common ugly URL format looks like:

randomexample.com/site/index.php?p=12345&ref=facebook.

Long URLs are also discouraged. For example, this would be undesirable:

randomexample.com/seo-tips-that-will-blow-your-mind-and-boost-your-serps-forever.

Guidance from Google suggests that the first few words in a page address are the most important. The attention of search engines and human readers alike drops off rapidly after several words. Updates to search algorithms, such as Penguin, are rendering keyword stuffing obsolete.

On the other hand, keywords do still matter. After all, they are the phrases people are searching for. The key is content. Relevancy as judged by the search engines relies heavily on accuracy and "human friendly" presentation. This extends to URLs. Long, unfriendly URLs are undesirable. Short URLs with the target keyword are optimal.

3. Take your content beyond text.

Multimedia content is a key element of the online experience. Images and videos are important for user engagement and social media sharing. Take a look at a Facebook, or even Twitter, feed. Notice how images and videos are a key part of the presentation and even a fair share of the content shared. Use relevant pictures, screenshots, memes, and other visual content to help break up blocks of text, as well as encourage sharing and clicks. The SEO boost comes from improved user engagement and social media signals metrics.

4. Don't post links, curate.

External links often get a lot of attention in terms of placement, structure, and so on. On the other hand, the importance of link curation is often neglected. Your outbound links tell search engines and readers about your site. It also helps provide semantic context for search analysis, such as the difference between Apple the corporation and an apple orchard. The quality and number of links affects the perceived quality of your site. A good approximation is using 1-2 outbound links per 500 words. As many external links as possible should be to authority sites or sites with unique related information.

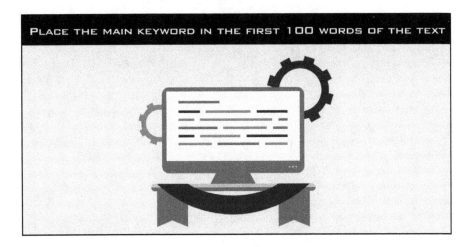

PLACE THE MAIN KEYWORD IN THE FIRST 100 WORDS OF THE TEXT

5. Get to the topic in the first 100 words

Human readers and search engine algorithms look to the lead of an article to tell them what it is all about. That means you should include your target keyword within the initial 100 words of a post. This is a typical habit for most writers, but many people start with a lot of introductory setup and/or fluff. Keep it simple and get to the point at the beginning.

6. Speed up your website.

Website loading time is an extremely important metric. It is one of a small handful of factors that Google has bluntly addressed. I highly recommend using GTMetrix and Google's PageSpeed Insights tools to review your rating and understand what needs improvement. The results will provide a detailed list of factors that impacted your result.

Two major factors impacting website loading speed are hosting and CDN usage. A quality host is important. While many shared hosts can offer rock bottom prices, they cannot offer the reliability and speed necessary for good SERPs. CDNs are cloud services that help relieve the server demands of a site.

7. Cultivate page authority and PageRank.

PageRank is like what other websites think of your page. Google measures this by the number and authority of inbound links. If you have a lot of low quality links, your SERPs will suffer. If you have a decent number of high value links, your PageRank and placement will improve considerably. As the rating increases, the perceived authority gain of the page increases the chances of hitting or holding a top 10 first page result.

USE H1 TAG FOR THE TITLE OF THE PAGE

8. Use the headline tag.

If you are using a content management system like WordPress or Drupal, chances are that your page titles already appear with an H1 tag. However, some website themes may override default options and some add-ons may also change rendering behavior. It is important to trust that you site installation is working as intended, but verify. Check your rendered web page's code to ensure the tag is appearing. If not, edit the page and enclose the post title with the H1 tag. The headline tag reinforces the topic for search engines and readers alike.

9. Google's Domain Authority metric is important.

Domain Authority is a measure of the general quality of a website overall. Pages on a site with a high DA will rank better than similar pages on weaker domains. Building a deep reserve of quality content, especially evergreen articles, is the most reliable way to improve this metric. Evergreen content maintains relevance over time. This can be by writing about a timeless topic or by recording an important part of history. They can also be periodically updated to stay timely and accurate. The depth of coverage is also a big factor. Having a lot to say relevant to the site's expertise indicates to search engines that it is authoritative and that visitors may find it informative and useful.

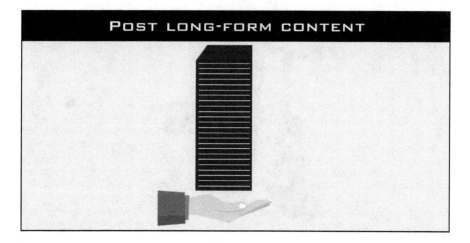

POST LONG-FORM CONTENT

10. Post long-form content.

Despite the stereotype of Internet users having a short attention span, the reality is that long content wins the days. A minimum length of 1000 words is where results improve. 2000+ words is the ideal goal. It establishes your site as an authority and it also organically targets several long tail and LSI keywords. SERPIQ studies and Upworthy reports indicate that link profiles and search results improves as content length grows above 1500 words. Some ghostwriters and copywriters state that this is because a good look at any given topic needs to be 1200+ words at bare minimum. On the upside, drilling down into a topic to find sufficient meat for this length means you will naturally include a lot of keywords and search relevance indicators.

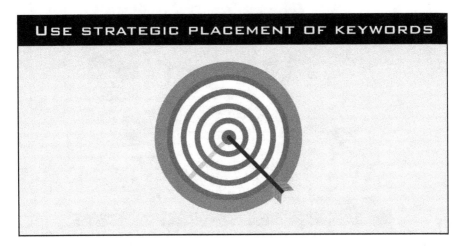

USE STRATEGIC PLACEMENT OF KEYWORDS

11. Use strategic placement of keywords and related topics.

Google and Bing have become hostile to keyword stuffing and SEO exploits. However, keywords are yet a crucial details. URL, title, and H-tag placement still matter. Long tail and LSI keywords communicate relevance and provide additional search visitors. The main difference is just filling in words no longer works. The keywords must be used organically in the text and they need to be anchored in strong content. Nevertheless, you must use keywords to tell search engines and readers what your site is all about and how it is relevant to searches.

12. Use modifiers that people use in searches.

This is really straightforward. Use the words you would expect people to use when searching. Examples include: "top 10", "the best", "tips", "how to", and "for business". These modifiers help define relevance for search engines and have proven popular in search engine results and on social media. Modifiers are great ways to build long tail keywords and attract visitors.

13. Make social media sharing easy.

Everyone is on Facebook, Twitter, Google+, and other social media these days. When you hear about something "going viral", you are hearing about something getting a lot of shares and clicks on social media websites. Make sure you tie in with prominent, well-placed social sharing buttons. Studies by SEO experts and BrightEdge show that making it easy to share your content with a few clicks drastically improves social media linking. Social media signals may not play a direct role in site ranking. On the other hand, they are a major source of traffic and backlinks, both of which do factor in to results placement.

14. Design your site for mobile access.

Google and Bing openly admit that responsive web design is a major factor in search placement. This is a reflection of a majority of Internet traffic originating from mobile phones and other devices. Google has stated that an alternate mobile design is suboptimal and Bing has stated that responsive web design gets preferential treatment. Ensure that your website has a unified theme that renders the proper version based on the operating system and browser of the visitor. Also, do not forget about the previous point on loading speed. A fast, clean browsing experience is even more important on mobile platforms.

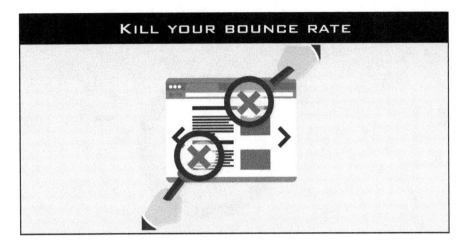

15. Kill your bounce rate.

Bounce rate is the SERPs killer that many site owners dread. It is how many users leave your page shortly after arrival. It is not everything, but it is a major factor for both search engine placement and user engagement. Build strong content. Use internal links near the beginning of posts. Link to related pages. Keep people on your site to improve conversions and get closer to the top results for your keyword. Pay attention to your link map to avoid sending users in circles or otherwise providing content that is too repetitive.

16. Keep users around.

While bounce rate measures how fast a user leaves, dwell time measures how long visitors stick around on a website. Many of the other points factor into this element. Long articles, engaging videos, and interesting image galleries will keep people on your site for some time. This way, even if they click back to the search engine results, you will be credited with a "long click" by Google. It is a signal to the search engines that your content was worth taking the time to read or watch. Avoid popups and other such tricks to artificially prevent visitors from leaving. It offends users and Google has been known to penalize such websites.

USE RELATED KEYWORDS AND SUBTOPICS

17. Mention related keywords and subtopics.

You may hear about latent semantic indexing (LSI) keywords. It sounds complicated, but it actually very simple. They are simply related keywords. You can see examples by typing keywords into Google Search and looking at the "Searches related to..." section at the bottom of the page. For example, if you have a page targeting "content marketing", "b2b content marketing" and "content marketing strategy" are both related keywords. Basically, it is a signal to Google that you are covering the subject in some depth and staying on-topic. You should also mention related keywords and subtopics. Using the same example of "content marketing", you may want to mention or include some information about "YouTube video development", "website ghostwriters", or "social media management". Talk about the things visitors want to know about and you will simultaneously let Google and Bing know that your content is authoritative and relevant.

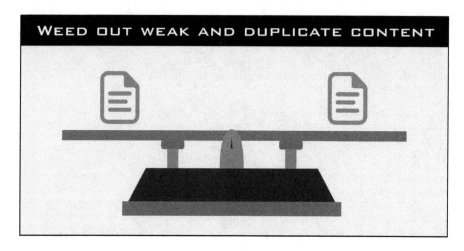

18. Weed out weak and duplicate content.

Set "noindex" on archive, category, and other navigation pages. Combine highly similar pages and/or rewrite old duplicate pages to refresh the content. Flesh out or delete "thin" pages that provide little useful information or purpose. There is a search engine penalty for thin and duplicate content. Make sure to build a decent library of strong articles to mitigate any possible remaining penalty and demonstrate site authority.

19. Content matters.

I know some people are tired of hearing content be hyped up, but it really is what matters now. It impacts visitor statistics, relevance signals, Chrome bookmarks, site authority, and other major SEO factors. While folks may debate the exact impact, there is no question that valuable unique content is crucial to stable, top placement SERPs. Google has also stated that it will be accounting for relevancy, accuracy, and topic coverage as it revises its search algorithms. Also, the sites that have fared best through all the changes in the search market, from the search providers to the methods of analysis they use, are those that have consistently published strong content. Wikipedia and Cracked.com are both excellent examples of how even imperfect sites can survive and thrive with the power of quality content.

20. Link to your own website.

Do not forget internal links! Wikipedia is the gold standard example. However, you should bear in mind that its internal link density matches its depth of content. Most sites should limit internal links to 2-5 per article. Sites with fewer pages should use fewer internal links, while those with many pages should use more internal links. It is a good way to boost the signal of old posts for readers and search spiders. Targets should be ideally relevant to the topic of the page or to the subtopic or related keyword used as anchor text.

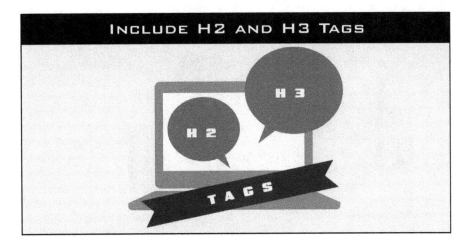

21. Use headings and subheadings.

They are not a major concern, but useful nevertheless. H2 and H3 tags are good ways to emphasize subtopics, as well as long tail and LSI keywords. They also break up the text a bit and improve readability. Create short, interesting, and topical subheadings for segments of your article and enclose them H2 or H3 tags. Research by Upworthy and other major sites shows that articles with headings and subheadings are read and shared more often. Social media discussion signals also tend to be stronger when pages incorporate this structural advice.

OPTIMIZE IMAGES

22. Optimize images.

While image search visitors have high bounce and leech rates, optimizing images is still important. It impacts regular SERPs and acts as a relevance signal for Google and Bing. The ideal is having an image with a file name include the target or a closely related keyword and alt text that includes the target or related keywords. Descriptions and captions are underutilized SEO opportunities. Use LSI and long-tail keywords in them to signal boost your page. Providing text data that search engines can interpret for images boosts the amount of targeted information it receives about the topic and relevance of a page.

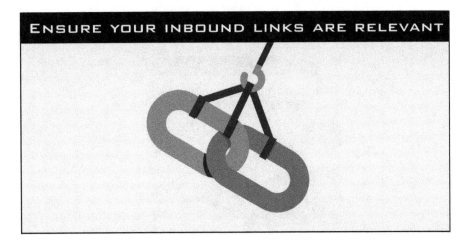

ENSURE YOUR INBOUND LINKS ARE RELEVANT

23. Ensure your inbound links are relevant.

Even when avoiding black hat spam, many link building packages result in a lot of high PR links but with very few relevant links. Google algorithm updates and Bing revisions have increasingly penalized sites with link profiles like that. Build links from relevant websites. If you sell car parts, links from a gaming forum or celebrity news blog are not going to help you with either targeted traffic or SERPs. On the other hand, a home mechanics' blog to linking to your site or posting auto parts for sale classifieds will boost your relevance and authority signals.

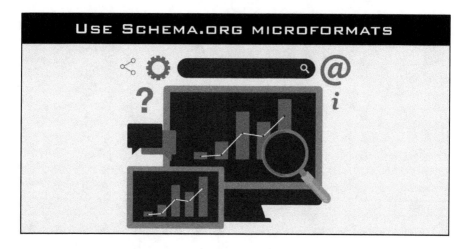

24. Schema.org microformats provide extra information to search engines.

Microformat data boosts SERPs. They also improve the amount and type of information shown in search results. Utilize them to maximize your communication with search spiders and improve your CTR. Be sure to set business information, ratings, and other such information.

The **Westin New York** Grand Central - TripAdvisor

www.tripadvisor.com › New York City Hotels ▾ TripAdvisor ▾

★★★★☆ Rating: 4 - 1,374 reviews - Price range: $$$

The **Westin New York** Grand Central, New York City: See 1374 traveler reviews, 573 candid photos, and great deals for The **Westin New York** Grand Central, ...

25. Use the tools that Google and Bing give you!

If you are not already using Google Webmaster Tools and Google Analytics, you should start right now. They are filled with statistics that Google gives you for free to help you improve your site. Using them can increase the speed and depth of indexing. The statistics provided also help provide direct evidence of user behavior, which is weighted by Google in results. You should also use Bing Webmaster Tools. While it drive less traffic than Google, it is still an important traffic source and Bind results provide additional signals for Google.

26. Use an XML sitemap.

Do not neglect to include an XML sitemap for your website. It provides a pre-made map of your website to search engine spiders, reducing the amount of resources needed to index your site and providing a modest SERPs boost. It also increases the chances that your search result will display additional pages on your website or offer the option to search for the keyword only on your website.

27. Use YouTube videos.

YouTube videos rank very well in search results. Some attribute this to Google's ownership of YouTube, but it is also true of other search engines. It is really the simple fact that YouTube gets a lot of clicks, has a low bounce rate and long dwell time, gets a lot of backlinks, and generally has fantastic user metrics from an SEO point of view.

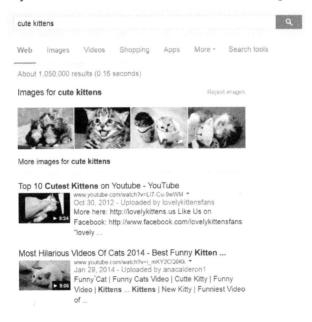

After the Google Panda and Penguin updates, YouTube has dominated Google's search results even more. Posting a few good videos with backlinks to your site can have a large impact.

TERMS OF USE STATEMENT AND PRIVACY POLICY

28. Don't forget the terms of use statement and privacy policy.

Search engines and standards organizations recognize that a terms of use statement and privacy policy are important elements of modern websites. They communicate trustworthiness to search engines and make usage conditions clear to visitors. They are especially important for sites that allow visitors to sign up, subscribe, or post. The standards demand that all such websites have easily found and readable terms & conditions and privacy policies.

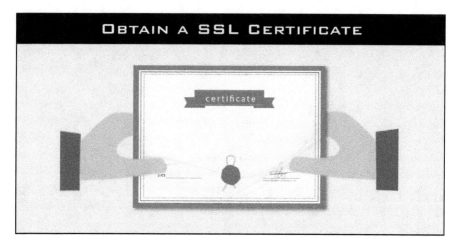

29. Build secure sites whenever possible.

SSL certificates are noted by Google and Bing. Sites that offer secure SSL connections are ranked higher. They also reassure users of the connection safety and privacy of their browsing. Properly configured SSL is especially vital for websites providing commercial transactions. It is a serious breach of consumer trust to use insecure connections for processing payments.

30. Leave breadcrumbs for your visitors.

Breadcrumb navigation is widely recommended. It is basically a menu that lets users move back up the site tree. It is considered very user and search spider friendly. You have probably seen it on a wide variety of sites.

You are here: Hostels ▶ Hostels Worldwide ▶ Australia Hostels ▶ Hostel Sydney ▶

Various SEO experts and search engine reporters have stated that breadcrumb navigation has a mild but positive impact on search placement. It is conventional wisdom among UI experts that it increases dwell time and improves the user experience. Most CMS packages have a wide variety of breadcrumb navigation plug-ins and modules, making it easy to choose one right for your site.

31. Reviews and reputation influencers impact your SERPs.

Yelp, Google Shopping, Yahoo Local, and other local, review, and shopping websites can substantively impact where you appear in search results. Having a number of reviews can make your local, company profile, and/or reviews show up early as extra results. Positive reviews also tell Google and Bing that your website is trustworthy and a relevant authority. Make sure you set up your local and review site profiles. Encourage your visitors to leave positive reviews for you with a targeted call to action.

BE USER FRIENDLY AND BREAK UP CONTENT

32. Be user friendly and break up content.

In addition to images and headers, also use bullet points and lists. They help prevent a wall of text effect. Google and Bing also show a preference for sites that use numbered lists and other ways of breaking up text into easily read and understood segments. Bullet points are good for short to medium sized lists and sets. Numbered lists are good for segments with accompanying text, steps, and ordered checklists.

33. Set canonical links.

Define canonical links on your website to avoid duplicate content penalties. You tell the search spiders which links are the "canonical" or most important ones. The other duplicate links are then treated as navigation aids and internal pages with no harm to search results. This is especially useful if you have multiple links pointing to the same page. As the most common example, you should define whether pages with or without "www" are the canonical version. This is because people will tend to link both. Similarly, it allows you to have a shortened URL link that redirects to the original content. Don't get penalized for fluffing out content when you can just define the canonical links.

Conclusion

Even if your business gets a certain number of customers who are not local to your brick-and-mortar store, making local SEO a priority is a no-brainer for every business owner who wishes to tap into their local market.

Regardless of your industry, an increasing number of your customers are using mobile and desktop devices to look for local businesses. This means you cannot afford to ignore the importance of optimizing your website for local search.

The information contained in this book is a jumping off point for you to start the work of optimizing your site. If you are not an SEO expert, don't worry. There are resources available that can help you cover the territory covered in this checklist.

The important thing to remember is that not optimizing your business for local search means that you will be missing out on opportunities to attract new customers. Businesses which rank in local searches see more conversions – and more sales – than businesses which don't.

If you would like the help of an expert Internet Marketing Specialist to get things going down the right path, do not hesitate to contact me.

I can be reached at (888) 95 BRUNO, and would love to discuss my ideas for helping you reach more local, targeted prospects online.

Bruno Pisano

(213) 842-0774 Direct

info@lav1.com

http://www.lav1.com

www.ingramcontent.com/pod-product-compliance
Lightning Source LLC
LaVergne TN
LVHW052313060326
832902LV00021B/3866